Why believe the Bible?

John Blanchard

EP BOOKS
1st Floor Venture House, 6 Silver Court,
Watchmead, Welwyn Garden City, UK, AL7 1TS
http://www.epbooks.org   sales@epbooks.org

EP Books are distributed in the USA by: JPL
Distribution, 3741 Linden Avenue Southeast,
Grand Rapids, MI 49548
E-mail: orders@jpldistribution.com
Tel: 877.683.6935

First published 2004
This edition 2016

**British Library Cataloguing in Publication Data
available**

ISBN 978-1-78397-172-5

Why Believe the Bible?

Setting the stage

Government agents had been on his trail for years, but he had always managed to evade them, slipping from one address to another under cover of darkness and with the help of sympathetic friends; but the net was closing in ...

Motivated by a hefty expense allowance from which he probably hoped to pocket a tidy balance as a reward, a special agent enrolled in a local university, wormed his way into all the right circles and eventually got on friendly terms with his target. Claiming one day that he had lost his purse, he persuaded his victim to buy him lunch in the local town—and even to lend him some money—but as they arrived at a pre-arranged eating place he gave an agreed signal to two waiting officers and his companion was arrested and flung into the state prison.

Eighteen months later, wasted and weakened by his confinement in a dark, foul-smelling cell infested with rats and other vermin, the prisoner was brought to trial. With everything already cut and dried before the court assembled, the sentence was a foregone conclusion. Two months later he was led out to the southern gate of the town, where a large pillar of wood in the form of a cross had been erected in an open space. A heavy chain hung from the top and a hemp noose was threaded through a hole in the upright. In front of a fascinated crowd that included a posse of local dignitaries, the prisoner's feet were tied to the upright, the iron chain clamped to his neck and the noose placed at his throat.

Piles of brushwood and logs were heaped around him, and then the executioner stepped forward. One brutal jerk on the noose and the prisoner's strangled body hung on the cross. One of the dignitaries lit the tinder, then sat back with the others to watch their victim burn. When they had seen enough an officer was ordered to cut the body down and let it fall into the blazing fire. The show was over, and the spectators left to get on with the rest of their day.

This happened early one morning in October 1536 (nobody is sure of the exact day) in the grounds of Vilvorde Castle, six miles north of Brussels. The victim's name was William Tyndale —but what was his crime? Treason? Threatening national security? Plotting to overthrow the government? Terrorism? Serial murder? None of the above! Officially, the long list of charges was said to amount to an indictment for heresy but, stripped of sophistry, the crowning 'crime' for which Tyndale was forced into exile and eventually hounded to death was this: *he translated a book from Hebrew and Greek into English*. Nor was it a book promoting anarchy, occultism, sedition, violence, or anything else likely to have an adverse effect on people's lives. Instead, it commended stable government, justice, peace, integrity and all the virtues one would wish to find in society. The book concerned was the Bible.

Tyndale's story is terrible but in no way unique and it is safe to say that no other book in history has been so hated, vilified and attacked. In the fourth century the Roman emperors Diocletian and Julian ordered their soldiers to destroy every copy they could find. In 1382 the first ever English translation faced vicious opposition and reading it was prohibited by law. When the first copies of Tyndale's work were smuggled back into England they were destroyed as 'pernicious merchandise'. In country after country it has been burned and banned and its translators persecuted, tortured and murdered. In recent times Marxist regimes, which at one stage dominated well over one-third of the world's population, mounted massive attacks on the Bible, destroying millions of copies in every nation they governed. Even in today's so-called tolerant age, the Bible remains a target of hatred and abuse. In some countries it is a criminal offence to sell or distribute it. Step off a plane with a Bible under your arm in these places and you would be in prison before you could reach Immigration.

Yet in spite of centuries of bitter opposition, the sheer volume of Bibles available today is mind-boggling. In 2015 the United Bible Societies distributed more than 34 million complete copies of the Bible. Count New Testaments, Gospels and other small Scripture publications and the total is almost 419 million copies.

The translation figures are equally impressive. 200 years ago the Bible, or a part of it, was available in just sixty-eight languages; by the end of 2014 this figure had risen to 2,883. These cater for well over 90% of the world's population, and translation projects are currently under way in more than 2,000 further languages.

Pulling all of this together invites some obvious questions. Why should the world's most despised book be in such overwhelming demand? What kind of publication could produce such diverse reactions? There is only one way to find out ...

The facts

Strictly speaking, the Bible is not a book at all, but a collection of sixty-six documents brought together over the course of about 1,500 years, the most recent dating from about AD95. The word 'Bible' is based on the Greek *biblos*, the inner bark of the papyrus plant. The Egyptians used papyrus (the root of our English word 'paper') as a form of writing material, largely because it was relatively cheap to produce and could be rolled up into large strips. *Biblos* eventually came to mean a written scroll, volume or book. There is nothing religious or spiritual about the word 'Bible'!

The Bible is divided into two parts, the Old and New Testaments. A 'testament' (or 'covenant') is a solemn and binding agreement. These two covenants show in two distinctive, but not contradictory, ways God's determination to bring men and women into a right relationship with himself. Grasping this will avoid the mistake of thinking that the Old Testament is out of date or that the New Testament is 'Plan B'. There is certainly a division in *time* between the two (there is a gap of 400 years between them) but not a division in *theme*. Both covenants are in complete agreement about the attributes and character of God, the nature of man and the way by which we can experience the reality of God's presence and power in our lives. The Old and New Testaments are like the two halves of a sentence: both are necessary before we can grasp the whole meaning. We can begin to clear away some major misconceptions about the Bible by listing some fundamental facts that most of its critics (and some of its supporters!) have never grasped.

Firstly, in Western versions of the Bible *the sixty-six documents* (I will call them 'books' from now on) *are not arranged in chronological order.* For example, in the Bible as we now have it, Hosea comes four books later than Jeremiah, but it was written about 150 years earlier, and James comes eight books from the end of the Bible, even though it may pre-date all but seven or eight of the twenty-six others in the New Testament. However, the first and last books are definitely in their right places, as the first (Genesis) begins with a description of how everything except God came into existence—including time, space and matter—while the last (Revelation) takes us beyond all future time and into eternity.

Secondly, *they were not all written in the same language.* Most were in Hebrew, many were in Greek and a few were in Aramaic, a version of an Afro-Asiatic language still in use today.

Thirdly, *the books are not all of the same kind.* Some are pure history; others concentrate on civil or criminal law; there are sections laying down rules and regulations about issues as diverse as temple worship and sanitation; parts are written as religious or lyrical poetry; there are large chunks of straightforward teaching; sometimes the writers have incorporated biography or autobiography; there is personal correspondence to individuals or groups of like-minded friends; there are poems, stories, speeches, prayers, hymns and sermons and also,

8

very importantly, there are long passages of prophecy (more of that later).

Fourthly, *in their original form the books had no chapter or verse divisions*. These slowly evolved over a period of some 700 years and the first complete Bible to contain our present chapter-and-verse divisions was the Geneva Bible, published in 1560.

Attacks

So much for the statistics, but it is when we get into the substance that the Bible comes under attack. Time and again I have heard it written off as 'a load of rubbish', or as 'myths' or 'folklore', but this kind of approach reminds me of the pre-election car bumper-sticker that read, 'My mind is made up. Please don't confuse me with facts.' Other attacks are not only more specific, but at first glance seem to make a fair point. These need to be faced and in this section we shall look at some of them, beginning with those that ask fundamental questions about the entire biblical text.

Corrupt copies?

The first attack asks, 'How do we know that the text of our present Bible is anything like the original?' This is a perfectly fair question. The original books were all handwritten on perishable material and until printing was invented in the fifteenth century all we had were manuscripts copied by hand again and again over hundreds of years. How do we know that these copies were anything like the originals? There are at least three important tests we can run on the Bible—and on other ancient documents.

Firstly, *how many documents do we have to work with*? The famous Dead Sea Scrolls, discovered from 1947 onwards, added 100 scrolls to the existing Old Testament documents, while we have well over 5,000 manuscripts of New Testament material in the original Greek and a total of some 20,000 sources to help us piece it all together. Other ancient works compare very badly. We have only nine or ten copies of Caesar's famous *Gallic War* (58–50BC), twenty copies of Livy's *Roman History* (59BC-AD17), seven copies of the histories of Pliny the Younger (c. AD61–113) and just two copies of *Histories and Annals* by Tacitus (c. AD55–120). The closest rival to the New Testament's 20,000 sources is Homer's famous *Iliad*, with just 643.

The Bible easily wins the numbers game, but this leads to a second test: *how close in time are the manuscripts we have to the original text?* In the Bible's case the oldest major manuscripts get to within 300 years or so, though two important papyri are 100 years closer, the famous *John Rylands Fragment* is thought to date from AD117–138 and three tiny fragments of papyrus in Magdalen College, Oxford, have been dated to the third quarter of the first century. Critics are quick to seize on these gaps as a reason for rejecting the Bible, yet ignore much bigger time-gaps for other documents which are accepted without question. Only one copy of Livy's *Roman History* gets closer than 400 years; with the works of Pliny the Younger the gap is 750 years; from Tacitus we have nothing closer than 900 years; and the oldest extant manuscript of Caesar's *Gallic War* dates from nearly 1,000 years after the events it describes.

No other known piece of ancient literature, religious or otherwise, can hold a candle to the Bible's credentials in this area. I recently visited some remains of Hadrian's Wall, which runs seventy-three miles across open country between the Solway Firth and the mouth of the River Tyne near the northern boundary of England. Nobody questions the fact that in AD122 the emperor Hadrian ordered the building of the wall to mark what was then the farthest extent of the Roman Empire—and 'to separate Romans from

Barbarians'. Nor does anybody question the fact that one of Hadrian's predecessors, Julius Caesar, first invaded Britain in 55BC, yet we now have only nine or ten manuscripts to support this and the earliest dates from over 900 years after the event.

The third test is in some ways the most important: *how can we be sure that the manuscripts were copied accurately?* Again, this is a perfectly fair question, but before answering it is worth pointing out that not even printing eliminates mistakes. One version, published in 1631, was known as 'The Wicked Bible' because the word 'not' was left out of the commandment, 'Thou shalt not commit adultery.' In 1717 another became known as 'The Vinegar Bible' because one passage was headed 'The Parable of the Vinegar' instead of 'The Parable of the Vineyard'. I still have a New Testament in which sailors trying to save their ship during a storm are said to have 'loosed the *rubber* bands', instead of 'the rudder bands'!

The much more serious question is whether, in the course of centuries of copying by hand, so many mistakes were made that we can no longer trust the text we have. There is no space here to go into detail, but the meticulous care with which the Jewish people copied their sacred Scriptures and the elaborate safeguards they put in place in an attempt to eliminate error almost defy belief. As a result, manuscripts dated hundreds of years apart are amazingly similar. To give one example, the Dead Sea Scroll manuscript of a particularly important chapter of the Bible is more than 1,000 years older than the earliest copy we previously possessed, yet of its 166 words only one (of three letters) is even in question, and the word concerned makes no material difference to the meaning of the passage. No other ancient document approaches anywhere near this amazing degree of consistency. In the *Mahabharata*, the national epic of India, about 10% of the lines are corrupt, while Homer's *Iliad* has twenty times more instances than the Bible in which the original words are in doubt. This is hugely significant yet in 100 scrolls representing all but one of the Old Testament's thirty-nine books and some 20,000 fragments of Scripture copied over a period of over 1,000 years we have only trivial differences. Sir Frederic Kenyon had no doubt what this means: 'It cannot be too strongly asserted that in substance the text of the Bible is certain: especially is this the case with the New Testament. The number of manuscripts from it, and of quotations from it of the oldest writers in the church, is so large that it is practically certain that the true reading of every doubtful passage is preserved in one or other of these ancient manuscripts. *This can be said of no other ancient book in the world*' (emphasis added).

Miracles

In the eighteenth century the Scottish sceptic David Hume launched a fierce onslaught on miracles. In a nutshell, his argument was that the laws of nature were based on the highest degree of probability, whereas miracles had the lowest degree of probability; so the wisest thing was not to believe in miracles. He even went on to say that the only miracle was that *anyone* should believe in them! One dictionary describes a miracle as 'an event or act which breaks a law of nature', and for many people this clinches the case: *in the absence of God*, anything that seems to contradict the scientific laws governing our world of time and space cannot be genuine and must have some other explanation. Notice the words I have emphasized! Once God is ruled out of the picture, events classified as miracles can be shrugged off as 'mysteries' or 'misleading' and, as its opening words are 'In the beginning God created the heavens and the earth', this would get the Bible off to the worst possible start!

One writer has identified 232 biblical miracles, but this gives nothing like the complete picture, as the Bible says that many others are unrecorded. If miracles never happen the Bible would self-destruct, but the right approach is not to begin by assuming the answer in advance, but by asking, '*Did* miracles happen?', and then examining each case in the light of the evidence. If the evidence does point to a miracle it demands an explanation, and to rule God out before considering that he might provide this is neither wise nor honest.

Dismissing miracles as non-events because they are against the laws of nature may seem a very 'scientific' thing to do, but the truth is exactly the opposite. The laws of nature never cause *anything*; they are merely our assessment of how things normally happen, and the person who believes in God claims that *they describe what God normally causes to happen*. The question of miracles is not a scientific question at all, but a theological one. If God exists, and determines the laws of nature, he himself is not subject to them and can override them whenever he chooses to do so.

In a letter to *The Times* in 1984 thirteen prominent scientists, most of them university professors, quietly eliminated one of the main arguments on the issue of miracles: 'It is not logically valid to use science as an argument against miracles. To believe that miracles cannot happen is as much an act of faith as to believe that they can happen … miracles are unprecedented events. Whatever the current fashions in philosophy or the revelations of opinion polls may suggest, *it is important to affirm that science … can have nothing to say on the subject*' (emphasis added). Rejecting the Bible because it records miracles is simply a non-starter.

'But science says ...'

The advances made by science and technology in the past 200 years have been breathtaking, and riding the crest of this wave is exhilarating. Medicine, communication, transportation and scores of other areas of modern life are being transformed as our scientific knowledge increases and technology harnesses it to bring huge benefits to our lives.

This phenomenal progress has led many people to make extraordinary claims for science. Philosopher Bertrand Russell wrote, 'Whatever knowledge is attainable must be attained by scientific means; and *what science cannot discover, mankind cannot know*' (emphasis added). Peter Atkins went even further and said, 'There is no necessity for God because science can explain everything.' If statements like these are correct, the Bible's credibility is sunk without trace—*but are they correct?* At least four things can be said.

Firstly, *science is an ongoing process of learning* in which from time to time things once claimed to be true are later found to be false. Scientist and philosopher Karl Popper goes so far as to say,

'Every scientific statement must remain tentative for ever.' In true science, the latest word is not necessarily the last word!

Secondly, *many things are beyond the reach of science and the scientific method*. Science cannot tell us why the world came into being, why the laws of nature are in place, why human beings are persons rather than what someone called 'computers made of meat', how to distinguish between right and wrong, why the mind exists, or why we have a spiritual dimension. It has no answer to life's biggest questions, those concerning meaning and purpose, death and human destiny. In addition (and relating directly to the issue we are discussing) *science cannot prove that God does not exist*. Peter Atkins was honest enough to begin his contribution a debate by saying, 'I have to admit from the outset that science cannot disprove the existence of God.'

Thirdly, *no scientific **fact*** (as opposed to a scientific theory) *has proved any biblical statement to be wrong*, while many such claims have had to be withdrawn. To give just one example, the Bible contains many references to the Hittites, a polytheistic people who occupied the region extending from northern Palestine to the Euphrates and who flourished for many centuries. When years of archaeology failed to turn up any signs of them, sceptics claimed that the Bible's record was either fiction or folklore— but later exploration uncovered masses of evidence confirming the Bible's record in great detail, and an entire museum in Ankara, Turkey, is now devoted to Hittite relics.

Fourthly, *many of the world's history-making scientists had no hesitation in endorsing the Bible*. These included the physicist Robert Boyle, the father of modern chemistry; chemist Michael Faraday, who discovered electromagnetic induction; astronomer Johannes Kepler; biologist Carolus Linnaeus, the father of biological taxonomy; natural physicist James Clerk Maxwell, the father of modern physics, who first predicted the existence of radio waves; naturalist Niels Steno, the founder of modern geology; and physicist William Thomson, who established the Kelvin Scale of absolute temperatures. Quotations from two other scientific giants drive the point home. The first is Sir Francis Bacon, philosopher, politician and eventually Lord Chancellor, who also made a powerful impact in scientific circles, especially in proposing a new theory of scientific knowledge that became known as the scientific method, stressing the importance of observation and experiment. A devout Bible student, Bacon wrote, 'There are two books laid before us to study, to prevent our falling into error; *first, the volume of the Scriptures, which reveal the will of God*; then the volume of the Creatures [Bacon meant the natural world] which expresses his power' (emphasis added). The second is the British mathematician and physicist

Sir Isaac Newton, who was elected President of the Royal Society for twenty-four successive years, the first person ever knighted for his services to science and most popularly known for his discovery of the law of universal gravitation. Like Bacon, he was also an avid student of Scripture and after years of diligent study came to the conclusion that the Bible was 'a rock from which all the hammers of criticism have never chipped a single fragment'.

Today, thousands of scientists, many of them prominent in their chosen discipline, are in complete agreement with these giants of the past and find no problem in reconciling their knowledge of science and Scripture. To say that science has proved the Bible wrong is to swim against a powerful tide of intelligent testimony.

Out of touch?

Millions of people take this line, brushing the Bible aside as being irrelevant in our modern world, but I am amazed that anyone should do this, as the Bible marries right in to today's media headlines.

For example, the Bible has a great deal to say, directly or indirectly, about marriage, divorce, remarriage, alcoholism, substance abuse, stress and depression. It speaks to man's most damaging emotions, such as anger, guilt, fear, doubt and anxiety, and condemns dishonesty, immorality, arrogance, greed, selfishness and obscenity. It addresses issues such as violence, murder, war and natural disasters. Are these irrelevant? It sets out clear principles that relate to moral and ethical issues today, such as abortion, euthanasia, homosexuality, human cloning and other forms of genetic engineering. Are these not contemporary issues?

The Bible teaches extensively on stable family life, the proper enjoyment of sex, employers' (and employees') responsibilities, social justice, business integrity and personal finances. It shows how to cope with poverty, sickness, rejection, bereavement and other personal traumas. To quote directly, it also points the way to 'love, joy, peace, patience, kindness, goodness, faithfulness, gentleness and self-control'. Are these of no importance to us?

It directly addresses animal welfare and the care of the environment. It speaks powerfully about the 'haves' and the 'have-nots' and emphasizes our duty to help the sick, the disabled, the bereaved, the poor, the homeless and the dispossessed, sometimes pinpointing widows and orphans. Can we sweep this aside?

Critics sometimes condemn the Bible as being 'negative' rather than constructive, but this is a false contrast. For instance, it is true that eight of the famous Ten Commandments begin with the words 'You shall not'—but does that mean that they are not constructive? Suppose your doctor prescribed some very powerful pills to deal with a serious sickness, that the prescription called for one to be taken every day for thirty days and that the container was clearly labelled, 'It is dangerous to exceed the stated dose.' This is undoubtedly a negative command, and your pharmacist might well underline it by warning you that an overdose could prove fatal. If you decided that your presence at work was so important that you would ignore the warnings and take all thirty pills as soon as you got home, your absence from work might well prove to be permanent! The negative command was not intended to harm you, but to do exactly the opposite—and the same is true of the Ten Commandments. 'You shall not murder' is negative, but obeying it preserves human life; 'You shall not commit adultery' is negative, but obeying it preserves the sanctity of marriage; 'You shall not steal' is negative, but obeying it safeguards personal property; 'You shall not give false testimony' is negative, but obeying it maintains integrity in our dealings with others.

The Bible goes even further. It addresses the greatest questions we ever face as human beings. Towards the end of his life the renowned French artist Pierre Gaugin settled in Tahiti, where he painted a vast canvas said to represent his last testament. In the top left-hand corner he wrote (in French), 'Where do we come from? What are we? Where are we going?' Despairing of finding answers, he then tried to commit suicide before dying in agony five years later from the effects of a sexually transmitted disease. Gaugin asked the right questions, but never found the answers, yet the Bible gives them, clearly and coherently. Irrelevant? Far from it! No other book ever written comes close to the way in which the Bible speaks to life in the twenty-first century.

Other roads up the mountain?

Another common argument for rejecting the Bible is to say that it is only one among many 'sacred writings' and that they may all be equally valid. Yet even a passionate atheist like Bertrand Russell squashed this idea: 'I think all the great religions of the world—Buddhism, Hinduism, Christianity, Islam and Communism—both untrue and harmful. *It is evident as a matter of logic that, since they disagree, not more than one of them can be true*' (emphasis added).

Russell's last sentence hit the nail on the head, as the world's major religions are defined, not by their similarities, but by their differences. They can obviously agree on how to deal with certain social and moral issues, but they are poles apart on the most important matters, and most of all on the nature of God himself. In Christian teaching the one true God exists in three equally divine persons and his essential nature is love, while Islam's God is singular and distant, and Sikhism's is remote and impersonal. Hinduism says there are millions of gods; Zoroastrianism says there are two, and in Buddhism there are none. How can all of these religions be 'different paths to the same summit', as many people claim, when they disagree on the nature of the summit? In 1996 Prince Charles announced that in the event of his succession to the British throne he would see himself as 'defender of faith' rather than as 'defender of *the* faith', but as the *Daily Telegraph*'s Janet Daley pointed out, 'You cannot defend all faiths—at least not at the same time—because each has beliefs that render those of the others false.' By the same token, it is illogical to equate the Bible with other 'sacred writings'.

Mistakes?

A friend sent one of my books to his brother, a militant atheist, hoping that it might influence him to change his position. The reply he received began: 'Anything that Blanchard writes is a load of total garbage, piffle, poppycock and unmitigated balderdash.' I can hardly claim to be infallible, but I did think this was a bit strong! What can be said to those who attack the Bible in the same way?

I usually begin by saying, 'If it is full of mistakes, come back in an hour's time and show me a dozen.' So far, nobody has risen to the challenge. This is hardly surprising, because one of the many remarkable things about the Bible is the way in which its statements are confirmed by external evidence. Although the Bible is not a history book it does contain a great deal of historical data and *whenever it has been possible to check this against contemporary evidence the Bible has been found to be accurate*. There is no space here to develop this point, but four distinguished experts will help us set the record straight.

Robert Dick Wilson, one-time Professor of Semitic Philology (the language and literature of the Middle East) at America's Princeton Theological Seminary, set himself a staggering forty-five-year study schedule, concentrating especially on Old Testament material. After exhaustive research into the Bible's record of about forty kings who had lived over a period of some 1,600 years, he came to the conclusion that while there were errors in other records, the Bible data was perfect and that mathematically *it is one chance in 750,000,000,000,000,000,000,000,000 that this accuracy is mere circumstance*. Weighing this up, he added, 'No stronger evidence for the substantial accuracy of the Old Testament record could possibly be imagined than this record of kings.'

William F. Albright, recognized as the world's greatest expert in Oriental studies, was Director of the American School of Oriental Research at Johns Hopkins University in Jerusalem, the author of over 800 books and articles, and the man whose verdict confirmed the authenticity of the Dead Sea Scrolls. In 1958 he wrote, 'Thanks to modern research we now recognize its substantial historicity. The narratives of the patriarchs, of Moses and the exodus, of the conquest of Canaan, of the judges, the monarchy, exile and restoration, *have all been confirmed and illustrated to an extent that I should have thought impossible forty years ago*' (emphasis added).

Sir William Ramsay was universally acknowledged to be one of the world's greatest archaeologists ever. A founder member of the British Academy, he originally went along with the trendy idea that the New Testament was largely mythology, rather than an accurate, contemporary historical record. For example, he was convinced that the book of Acts, written by the author of the Gospel attributed to Luke, a first-century physician, was nothing more than folklore cobbled together by an anonymous storyteller centuries after the events it claimed to record. Yet after painstaking on-site research Ramsay became convinced that Luke's data was so precisely accurate that he should be recognized as 'a historian of the first rank' who 'should be placed along with the very greatest of historians'.

Nelson Glueck, the world's foremost biblical archaeologist, excavated over 1,000 sites in the Middle East, including the copper mines of King Solomon and the ancient Red Sea port of Ezion Geber. After years of meticulous research, he wrote of 'the almost incredibly accurate historical memory of the Bible and particularly when it is fortified by archaeological fact', and went so far as to say, 'It may be stated categorically that *no archaeological discovery has ever controverted a biblical reference*' (emphasis added).

These are world-class testimonies and even if they do not of themselves prove that every historical statement in the Bible is true, they make nonsense of the cavalier claim that the Bible is 'full of mistakes'.

Contradictions?

A variation of the previous attack is to claim that the Bible is full of contradictions. From dates to doctrine, geography to genealogy and names to numbers, critics have claimed that the Bible often contradicts itself and can therefore be rejected out of hand, but I have yet to meet anyone able to prove this. Of the many *supposed* contradictions, here are a few examples, together with the response that can be made to them.

1. Josiah, the King of Judah, is said to have 'walked in all the ways of his father David', yet we know that Josiah was not the son of David but of Amon. This looks like a glaring contradiction—until we realize that in Old Testament times it was common for historians to shorten genealogies in this way. There is no Hebrew word for 'grandson', so the only way to refer to a grandson many times removed was either to list all the fathers that came between or miss them out and call him 'son'.

2. King David's son Absalom is said to have had three sons, but later he is recorded as saying, 'I have no son to carry on the memory of my name.' This apparent contradiction is easily answered by assuming that all three sons had died by the time Absalom made his lament.

3. Jesus said that his body would lie in the grave for 'three days and three nights', but the Bible tells us that he was buried on the day preceding the Jewish sabbath (a Friday) and rose from the dead on the first day of the week (Sunday). This seems to be a serious flaw, but it misses the point that the Jews counted any part of a day as 'a day', so that in this case one complete day (Saturday), parts

of two other days (the Friday and the Sunday) and the two intervening nights would commonly be referred to as 'three days and three nights'.

4. One New Testament writer says that on the first Easter Day two angels appeared at the tomb of Jesus, while another only mentions one angel. Critics have pounced on this, but common sense alone tells us that if there were two angels it is mathematically certain that there was one. If the second writer had said there was *only* one angel the critics would be in a strong position, but the text as it stands leaves them without a case.

5. The Bible says that Jesus will one day return to the earth and that at the precise moment when he appears 'two men will be in the field', which seems to mean that this will be during daylight hours. Yet elsewhere Jesus spoke of his return as being 'on that night' when 'two people will be in one bed'. This looks like an obvious error, until we remember that the middle of the day in one part of the world is the middle of the night in another.

Not everything in the Bible is as clear as daylight and not every alleged contradiction can be answered as easily as these. Nor would it be sensible to claim that over many centuries of copying the Scriptures by hand there had never been a slip of the pen. Yet years of careful study show that these are few and far between, almost entirely confined to six of the Old Testament's historical books, and are just tiny discrepancies in numbers or an occasional word. Even more importantly, *not even one of these 'slips of the pen' makes a material difference to the meaning or significance of the passage concerned.*

Five more things need to be said before we end this section of the booklet.

Firstly, *an unanswered question is not the same as proof of a mistake* and an unsolved problem is not necessarily an error.

Secondly, when textual criticism was at its height about 150 years ago scores of alleged errors and discrepancies were being touted, *but patient research has steadily whittled away at these*, and theologian R. C. Sproul claims, 'There is less reason today to believe that the Bible is full of contradictions than at any time in the history of the church.'

Thirdly, it has been accepted for over 2,500 years that, with certain qualifications, *the benefit of the doubt must be given to the document concerned.* Simon Greenleaf, Royal Professor of Law at Harvard University, was one of the world's greatest experts on legal evidence. At one stage in his life he set out to debunk the credibility of the New Testament, but eventually came to the conclusion that it was utterly reliable and that 'the attributes of truth are strikingly apparent throughout the Gospel histories'. Greenleaf's first rule of documentary criticism was this: 'Every document apparently ancient, coming from the proper repository or custody, and bearing on its face no evident marks of forgery, *the law presumes to be genuine and devolves on the opposing party the burden of proving it to be otherwise*' (emphasis added). This puts the ball firmly back in the critic's court.

Fourthly, 200 years of determined attacks seem to have left the Bible unscathed. At the end of 1974, TIME magazine ran an article entitled, 'How true is the Bible?' and came to this conclusion: 'The breadth, sophistication and diversity of all this biblical investigation are impressive, but it begs a question: Has it made the Bible more credible or less? ... After more than two centuries of facing the heaviest scientific guns that could be brought to bear, the Bible has survived—and is perhaps better for the siege. *Even on the critics' own terms—historical fact —the Scriptures seem more acceptable now than they did when the rationalists began the attack*' (emphasis added).

Fifthly, the person prepared to brush all of this aside and to challenge the Bible's integrity and authority can properly be invited to ask the following questions: 'Is my opposition to the Bible fuelled by prejudice or principle? Do I have expert knowledge of the three languages

(Hebrew, Greek and Aramaic) in which the Bible was originally written? Do I have a clear grasp of the context in which each book was compiled? Do I have a correct understanding of every passage and of the sense in which the writer used words or numbers? Can I in every case identify the author's use of language, so that I can determine whether he was employing metaphor or hyperbole, or using a simile or a localized idiom? Am I certain as to whether any given passage is an allegory, a parable or a factual narrative? Do I understand the significance of every one of the religious and civil laws and customs of all the times and places covered by the Bible's writers? Am I certain that no amount of textual or archaeological research will shed any further light on any of the issues concerned? Am I honestly open to being convinced that the Bible really *is* the Word of God and that it speaks to me?' Any individuals who can truthfully answer 'Yes' to all of these questions, or who feel that they have some other reliable authority on which to base their rejection of the Bible, may feel qualified to press on with their attack. If not, surely it would be wiser—and humbler—to try a different approach.

Defence

When the nineteenth-century British preacher Charles Spurgeon was being encouraged to defend the Bible, he replied, 'Defend the Bible? I would sooner defend a lion! Let it loose!' This was typical Spurgeon, but 'defence' is a perfectly good word to describe what we find when we open the Bible and let it speak for itself.

All together

As we saw earlier, the Bible is not so much a single book as a 'library' of sixty-six separate documents written by some forty authors at intervals stretching over more than 1,500 years. They included a king, a statesman, a governor, a civil servant, a doctor and at least two fishermen, as well as a tent-maker and several of whom we know nothing but their names. They lived in vastly different times and places and only a few ever met any of the others. We can assume that if asked about any controversial subject other than religion they would have had as many different opinions as we might expect to hear on a media chat show. Yet without any collaboration or spin-doctoring, they have given us a body of writing that is amazingly coherent.

Commenting on this, J. I. Packer says, '(The Bible has) an organic coherence that is simply stunning. Books written centuries apart seemed to have been designed for the express purpose of supplementing and illuminating each other ... Truly, the inner unity of the Bible is miraculous: a sign and wonder challenging the unbelief of our sceptical age.' This is hardly proof that the writers were all telling the truth, yet, as truth unites and error divides, how else could everything they wrote fuse so perfectly together? The unity of the Bible is so amazing that one could be forgiven for thinking that all its writers were speaking with one voice—*or is this the whole point?* ...

Their Master's voice

If we 'let it loose' as Spurgeon recommended, the one overwhelming message that comes across loud and clear is the Bible's claim that *it is nothing less than the Word of God*. In the Old Testament, seventeen of its thirty-nine books major on prophecy and seventeen on history, while the remaining five are poetry. The prophets had no hesitation in claiming that when speaking in prophetic mode they were acting as God's mouthpieces and that their message was to be treated as coming directly from him—and the same claim runs through all the other books.

Phrases like 'God said', 'God spoke', and 'the word of the Lord came' occur some 700 times in the first five (historical) books alone and some forty times in one chapter. In the Old Testament as a whole there are nearly 4,000 direct claims to divine authorship. No other literature known to man makes such clear, consistent and dogmatic claims.

We see the same kind of thing in the New Testament. The apostle Paul, who wrote at least thirteen of its twenty-seven books, not only described the Old Testament as 'the very words of God', but made no bones about the authority of his own writings: *If anybody thinks he is a prophet or spiritually gifted, let him acknowledge that what I am writing to you is the Lord's command* (1 Corinthians 14:37). Elsewhere, he commended those who received his message *not as the word of men, but as it actually is, the word of God* (1 Thessalonians 2:13), insisting that he was God's mouthpiece, responsible not for devising the message, but for delivering it.

Other New Testament contributors said the same thing. The apostle Peter had no hesitation in claiming that his own writing came *from heaven* (1 Peter 1:12). The apostle John, another New Testament heavyweight, began the last book in the Bible by saying that what he was about to write was *the word of God* and signed off by assuring his readers that his words were *trustworthy and true*, having come to him directly *from the Lord, the God of the spirits of the prophets* (Revelation 1:2, 22:6).

The Bible's most concise claim to its divine authorship is to say, *All Scripture is God-breathed* (2 Timothy 3:16). God-breathed perfectly translates the original Greek adjective, *theopneustos*, from the noun *theos* (God) and the verb *pneo* (to breathe). This tells us, not that the writers were inspired, but that what they wrote had been expired—that God 'breathed out' the very words they wrote down. As Peter himself put it when referring to Old Testament writings, *Prophecy never had its origin in the will of man, but men spoke from God as they were carried along by the Holy Spirit* (2 Peter 1:21).

Critics quickly jump in at this point: 'To say that the Bible is the Word of God because it says it is the Word of God is to argue in circles.' This may sound as if it clinches the argument, but at least four things can be said in reply.

Firstly, we are all familiar with *the idea of appealing to higher authority*. In England, serious crime is tried in the Crown Court and a person convicted there could appeal on a point of law to the Criminal Division of the Court of Appeal. If this appeal failed, it could then be taken to the Supreme Court. This is the final court of appeal in the UK for civil cases, and for criminal cases in England, Wales and Northern Ireland, but the case could be taken one step further, to the

European Court of Human Rights. But that is the end of the road, as English law recognizes no higher authority. In philosophy and religion the same point is inevitably reached.

Secondly, *all claims for absolute authority have such authority built in, or they could not be sustained.* For example, those who believe that human reason is the ultimate authority must look to human reason as the basis for claiming this to be the case. This is circular reasoning—but how can it be avoided? The same is true of those who claim that logic or science has absolute authority; only by presupposing what they are claiming can their claim be made. (The only people who avoid this are hard-line sceptics, but they end up in hopeless confusion because if they are absolutely consistent they must be sceptical of the very scepticism on which they insist!)

Thirdly, we have already seen that *the Bible is no ordinary book.* Tested in every way possible, its integrity remains intact, with witnesses such as history, geography and prophecy providing impressive supporting evidence. This evidence is so solid that it is at least reasonable to suppose that the Bible can also be trusted when it speaks thousands of times about its own origin. The Bible is the only book we know that claims from cover to cover that it is God's direct, verbal message to man, and theologian John Frame is not exaggerating when he says, 'If God's speech has an obvious location that location must be in the Holy Scriptures. There is simply no other candidate.' With its impeccable track record, it is unreasonable and illogical to charge it with making thousands of false and blasphemous statements about its own authorship—and to do so without any evidence to back up the charge. Trying to avoid the Bible's central claim is like trying to avoid an avalanche by dodging individual stones. The Bible gives us many impressive reasons for believing that it is exactly what it claims to be—*the living and enduring word of God* (1 Peter 1:23).

Fourthly, if God created all reality outside of himself and has sovereign authority over all of creation, how could he turn to a greater authority to authenticate his own existence, attributes or purposes? The Bible makes this very point in recording how God affirmed a covenant with the Old Testament patriarch Abraham: *Since there was no one greater for him to swear by, he swore by himself* (Hebrews 6:13). As the fourth-century theologian Hilary of Poitiers commented, 'Only God is a fit witness to himself.' By the same token, if the Bible is the Word of God, how can it possibly point us to any higher authority in order to authenticate its claims?

Some people try to find a middle road by saying that although the Bible is not the Word of God it is a highly moral book, with much to teach us, but this idea never gets off the ground. If the Bible were not the Word of God, yet claimed that it was, it would be the most dangerous, blasphemous and contemptible book ever written, lying to us about our origin, giving us a false basis for human dignity, faking a framework for the meaning and purpose of life and cruelly hoodwinking us about what lies beyond the grave. Calling the Bible a good book but not 'God's book' lacks even basic logic.

The Master's verdict

As we shall see later, the Bible's message ultimately centres on the person and work of Jesus of Nazareth. This is hardly surprising, as careful researchers have pointed out that Scripture applies to Jesus every major name, attribute and title of God. If Jesus spoke with divine authority, his assessment of the Bible would be the best possible endorsement of its claims—and we are not left guessing as to what his assessment was. The only 'Bible' Jesus had in his day was the Old Testament, but he is recorded as quoting verbatim from it nearly forty times (from thirteen different books) in the course of his teaching, and as referring to it on many other occasions. How did he rate it?

Firstly, he accepted without question that its history was reliable. He used at least fifteen events recorded in the Old Testament to illustrate spiritual truth about issues such as marriage, family relationships, miracles, the final judgement, heaven and hell.

Secondly, it was the only body of teaching to which he ever gave his approval and he acknowledged its unchangeable authority on every subject it addressed, telling his listeners, *The Scripture cannot be broken* (John 10:35).

Thirdly, he was so concerned that it should be properly understood that he frequently corrected those who were misinterpreting or abusing it.

Fourthly, he claimed that the entire Old Testament was a prophetic prelude to his own coming into the world; to give just one example, he pinpointed the three major divisions of the Old Testament and said, *Everything must be fulfilled that is written about me in the Law of Moses, the Prophets and the Psalms* (Luke 24:44). Jesus saw himself as the key to understanding everything the Old Testament said.

Fifthly (and the only point we need to emphasize here), he made it crystal clear that he accepted the entire Old Testament as being the Word of God. Challenging those who questioned life beyond the grave, he asked, *Have you not read what God said to you ...?* (Matthew 22:31) and then quoted words spoken by Moses. Attacking hypocrites who were misconstruing statements in two Old Testament books, he accused them of *setting aside the commands of God* (Mark 7:9).

Quoting from one of the Psalms, he said that David (the human author) was *speaking by the Holy Spirit* (Mark 12:36). As far as Jesus was concerned, what the Bible said, God said.

The future—now!

The next endorsement of the Bible's claim to be the Word of God raises a subject that fascinates millions of people—foretelling the future. A front-page headline in the *Daily Mail* made the eye-catching announcement that computer analysis of the Bible had discovered a hidden code 'that predicts every event in history'. The inside pages toned this down to read 'every major event in history', but it was still an amazing claim and did wonders for the paper's circulation figures. Journalist Michael Drosnin later pulled the material together and in *The Bible Code* claimed that man's first landing on the moon in 1969, the 1974 Watergate scandal that forced United States President Richard Nixon out of office, the collision in 1994 between the Shoemaker-Levi comet and the planet Jupiter, and the 1995 assassination of Israel's prime minister Yitzhak Rabin were all encoded in Bible passages written 3,000 years earlier.

Drosnin was soon debunked, especially when it was found that one could 'predict' other major events by applying the same computer-generated programme to books like *War and Peace* and *Moby Dick*!—but not before *The Bible Code* had become a short-lived best seller.

The sixteenth-century writer known as Nostradamus, wrote 942 four-line poems said to predict future events. He had an obsessive interest in astrology, clairvoyance and the occult, and his poems, written in a garbled mixture of five languages, are couched in such vague terms that they could be made to fit almost anything, from a stock-market crash to an outbreak of earthquakes, yet vast numbers of people still look to him for clues and he has nearly 850 pages on my favourite web-site search engine. The annual *Old Moore's Almanack*, first published in 1680 as *Vox Stellarum* (Voice of the Stars), still has a worldwide readership, yet a careful study of 200 high-profile astrologers' predictions in just one randomly chosen volume showed that less than five per cent materialized and that these could have been based on probability, inside knowledge or astute speculation.

In spite of these facts, the human appetite for knowing what lies ahead seems insatiable. Millions read horoscopes published in countless magazines and newspapers, while others look for clues in crystal balls, tea-leaves or tarot cards. Yet it is fairly safe to say that hardly any who do so realize two remarkable things about the Bible—firstly, that about thirty per cent of it consists of prophecy of one kind or another; and, secondly, that *not a single prophecy made according to its own criteria has ever been shown to be false*. Surely this ought to get our attention?

Although genuine Bible prophecy sometimes concerns individuals' health, daily needs and family affairs, it never descends to the trivial nonsense traded by today's cranks, charlatans and con artists, which is largely aimed at massaging people's feel-good factor. Most prophecies in Scripture involve issues of national or international importance and make dogmatic forecasts of future events, sometimes being quite specific about their timing, so that their accuracy could be checked. This would hardly be surprising if the prophets were God's spokesmen and were passing on information he had given them, but this raised an obvious problem: how were people to know whether those claiming to be prophets were genuine and that their words could therefore be trusted? This was the test: *If what a prophet claims in the name of the Lord does not take place or come true, that is a message the Lord has not spoken. That prophet has spoken presumptuously. Do not be afraid of him* (Deuteronomy 18:22).

This is very different from saying that if any given prophecy turned out to be right the person making it was a genuine prophet. Anybody might make a correct forecast from time to time (as football pundits and horse-racing tipsters do today) yet this was no proof of his credentials. Instead, *if even one prophecy turned out to be false the prophet's claim to be genuine was in shreds*. It was no good his pleading that he was 'only human' and so 'bound to get things wrong from time to time'. A true prophet always got it right, even when his prophecy seemed to be ridiculous. Sceptics sometimes suggest that the 'prophecies' were made after the events they predicted, but there are so many cases in which the dating rules this out that this attack is pointless.

But was there not some possibility, however remote, that people claiming to be God's prophets were nothing more than religious fanatics who 'just happened to get it right'? Peter Stoner answers the question by concentrating on just eleven prophecies taken from the writings of four prophets, Isaiah, Jeremiah, Ezekiel and Micah. These prophecies related to the land as a whole, the destruction of Jerusalem, the rebuilding of its temple and the later enlargement of the city—and they were all fulfilled to the letter. Calculating the probability of this happening by chance to be one in 8×10^{63}, Stoner illustrates what this means. He says that if we were to scoop together a pile of coins equal in size to 100 billion stars in each of two trillion galaxies in just one second, add to the pile at the same rate every second, day and night, for twenty-one years, then ask a blindfolded friend to pick out one coin from this incomprehensibly massive pile, his chances of doing so would be the same as the likelihood that these four prophets could have got their forecasts right by guesswork. This is impressive enough, yet these are just eleven prophecies out of several hundred recorded in the Old Testament alone. What must the odds be against all of them being guesswork? Writing about the evidence for what he calls 'God's fingerprints on the Bible', John Benton understandably says that its prophetic teaching is 'probably the most direct evidence for the special involvement of God with this book'.

Revolutions

A fourth reason for believing the Bible is its unique record in changing individual lives and entire societies for the better. In New Testament times the Christian church in Corinth included in its membership those who had been sexually immoral, idolaters, adulterers, male prostitutes, homosexual offenders, thieves, greedy, drunkards, slanderers and swindlers, yet all had been transformed by biblical truth. Since then, millions have added their testimony that the Bible's influence had revolutionized the moral qualities of their lives for the better.

On a wider scale, no identifiable group of human beings has had a more positive impact on their contemporary culture than those who have been motivated and directed by the Bible. They have founded countless schools, hospitals and charitable institutions and, as author John Stott has pointed out, their influence has been enormously beneficial in many other areas: 'They abolished the slave trade and freed the slaves, and they improved the conditions of workers in mills and mines and of prisoners in gaols. They protected children from commercial exploitation in the factories of the West and from ritual prostitution in the temples of the East. Today they bring leprosy sufferers both the compassion of Jesus and modern methods of reconstructive surgery and rehabilitation. They care for the blind and the deaf, the orphaned and the widowed, the sick and the dying. They get alongside junkies and stay alongside them during the traumatic period of withdrawal. They set themselves against racism and political oppression. They get involved in the urban scene, the inner cities, the slums and the ghettos, and raise their protest against inhuman conditions in which so many are doomed to live. They seek in whatever way they can to express their solidarity with the poor and hungry, the deprived and the disadvantaged.'

Nobody is suggesting that only Bible believers have been involved in such work, but their record is second to none. It has been calculated that 75% of the social revolution that swept Western society in the eighteenth and nineteenth centuries was driven by biblical teaching, with names like William Wilberforce (the abolition of slavery), Elizabeth Fry (prison reform), the Seventh Earl of Shaftesbury (improving the status and conditions of the mentally ill) and Thomas Barnardo (housing destitute children) among those who took leading parts. Today, countries where freedom, justice and tolerance are the norm are almost all influenced by the Bible's teaching, in stark contrast to those that have deliberately rejected it. *The Book of Knowledge* is not overstating the case when it says, 'Considered simply as literature, *apart from its religious associations*, the Bible, in every language, has made a deeper impression upon the human mind than any other book in the world, and *the extent to which it has shaped the world's ideas, and thus the world's history, cannot be estimated*' (emphasis added). Of course there have been cases (the notorious Crusades and Inquisitions in the Dark Ages and Middle Ages are terrible examples) in which religious leaders have grossly misapplied the Bible's teaching to justify appalling violence, but these are the exceptions that prove the rule, and the Bible's unparalleled influence for good is tremendously impressive.

Getting the message

R.C. Sproul says, 'If the Bible is trustworthy, then we must take seriously the claim that it is more than trustworthy,' and these few pages alone have given sufficient reason for believing the Bible to be the Word of God. Yet this is only the first step in responding to it as we should. It has not been given to us merely for our information, but for our transformation, so that, as its message grips our minds and changes our hearts, we might have a God-centred world-view and lifestyle.

But what is its message?

The first thing to grasp is that the Bible is not a haphazard collection of statements—not even of true and valuable statements. Every year the Gideons International place millions of Bibles in places such as hotels, hospitals, schools, colleges, universities and prisons, and these Bibles include guidelines on where to turn for help in times of particular need. These guidelines are carefully and sensitively chosen and many people have found life-changing help in following their advice, yet this is not the best way of 'getting the message'. The Bible is not a spiritual version of a trades directory, nor should we treat it as a 'lucky dip', sticking a pin in a page and trying to do whatever we read there. After all, three stabs could come up with: *So Judas ... went away and hanged himself, Go and do likewise*, and *What you are about to do, do quickly*. All three statements are taken directly from the Bible, but to rip them out of context and obey them to the letter would hardly be life-enhancing!

The biblical approach is to begin by realizing that it is a message about God and man and their relationship to each other. To use a modern phrase, the Bible has a meta-narrative (in ordinary language, a storyline). This is confirmed by its amazing harmony. In J. I. Packer's vivid illustration the Bible is like a symphony orchestra in which 'each instrument has been brought willingly, spontaneously, creatively to play his notes *just as the great conductor desired*, though none of them could ever hear the music as a whole' (emphasis added). It is not a vague amalgamation of ideas that came to self-styled religious gurus claiming mystical insight. Instead, its message is rooted in the lives of real men and women, from kings and queens to statesmen and civil servants, from soldiers to shepherds, from husbands and fathers to wives and mothers, all of them woven into the ebb and flow of historical events, many of which can be traced. In the space available here we can give only a very brief outline of what that message is, beginning with some of the many statements the Bible makes about the nature of God himself.

The nature of God

- God is unique: *There is no God but one* (1 Corinthians 8:4). All other 'gods' are figments of human imagination.

- God is personal, not a 'thing' such as cosmic dust or atmospheric energy. God thinks, chooses, makes promises, keeps them all and is *compassionate and gracious* (Psalm 86:15). It has been said that 'The ultimate fact about the universe is a personal God.' Although there is only one God, he exists in three persons, Father, Son and Holy Spirit, each one being fully divine, co-equally with the other two.

- God is spiritual, with no material dimensions such as a physical body; *God is spirit* (John 4:24).

- God is eternally self-existent, neither created nor brought into existence by any power or person. He is underived and independent, the *eternal God* (Romans 16:26) who is from *everlasting to everlasting* (Nehemiah 9:5).

- God is transcendent, over and above time, space and all other reality, *the one whom the heavens, even the highest heaven, cannot contain* (1 Kings 8:27).

- God is immutable: *he does not change like shifting shadows* (James 1:17).

- God is holy, utterly without flaws, blemishes, weaknesses, shortcomings or disabilities; in the Bible's vivid metaphor, *God is light; in him there is no darkness at all* (1 John 1:5)

- Finally, in the Bible's own words, *God is love*, (1 John 4:8) and all his actions, even those which seem to our limited understanding to be exactly the opposite, are expressions of his *unfailing love* (Psalm 6:4).

The origin of the universe

Moving into the Bible's storyline, we are told in its opening words that *In the beginning God created the heavens and the earth*. In the original Hebrew language there was no single word to describe the universe, and the expression 'the heavens and the earth' simply means all reality other than God himself, from asteroids to ants, time to titanium, mammoths to microbes, energy to elephants and gravity to grasshoppers. What is more, he did not create the universe out of any kind of pre-existing substance or essence, but created everything out of nothing: *The universe was formed at God's command, so that what is seen was not made out of what was visible* (Hebrews

11:3). Many people get in a tangle over the question of creation by concentrating on its *mechanism* rather than its *meaning*. The fact is that, however we try to manipulate the data, the Bible does not tell us exactly how or when creation took place. Instead, its focus is on the fundamental fact that *God ... made heaven and earth and sea and everything in them* (Acts 4:24).

The creation of man

Unlike anything else in the entire created order: *God created man **in his own image**, in the image of God he created him; male and female he created them* (Genesis 1:27).

The words I have emphasized pinpoint humanity's uniqueness. They have nothing to do with size, weight, shape, or any other material attribute, as God has none of these, but they explain why as humans we have *personality*—giving us powers of thought, feeling and will that go far beyond the brute instinct of purely animal life. Our creation 'in the image of God' also explains why we have a capacity to relate to God, to worship him and to live in fellowship with him.

The nature of man

When creation was complete, *God saw all that he had made, and it was very good* (Genesis 1:31). The 'all' included man, who was created to be *like God in true righteousness and holiness* (Ephesians 4:24). Yet he was not a robot. He was given free will and moral responsibility, and for an unspecified time (we have no idea how long) he chose to live in complete obedience to his Maker, and as a result enjoyed a perfect relationship with him and complete harmony with all the rest of creation.

At some point in history (and again we have no idea when) man chose for the first time to disobey God and to go his own way, and in that catastrophic moment, ... *sin entered the world through one man, and death through sin* (Romans 5:12). No words in the English language convey a more appalling and catastrophic fact. Our first parents' relationship with God was shattered; they lost their innocence and free will; their nature became infected with godless ideas, attitudes and affections; they knew what it was to feel guilty, alienated, ashamed, anxious and afraid; their inter-personal relationships were poisoned by suspicion, dishonesty and mistrust, and their bodies became subject to decay, disease and death.

Man's rebellion against his Maker had even wider repercussions. The entry of sin threw the whole created cosmos out of sync. The Second Law of Thermodynamics, which says that the universe is becoming increasingly disorganized, confirms the Bible's statement that it is now *in bondage to decay* (Romans 8:21). Natural disasters such as earthquakes, tornadoes and floods, unknown before sin entered the world, are now signs of sin's presence and effect.

As part of the human race, we all inherit our first parents' corrupt, sinful nature, with the result that even the best of us are by nature rightly exposed to the righteous anger of a holy God.

For many people this is the point at which they abandon any idea that the Bible might be telling the truth. Most sensible people will admit that they are not perfect, and accept the Bible's verdict that *All have sinned and fall short of the glory of God* (Romans 3:23). The sticking point comes when the Bible insists that we sin because we are sinners, that things such as *evil thoughts, sexual immorality, theft, murder, adultery, greed, malice, deceit, lewdness, envy, slander, arrogance and folly come from within, out of men's hearts* (Mark 7:21-22).

Yet nothing is more plainly taught in the Bible than what is sometimes called 'original sin'. King David of Israel, one of the most significant people in the Old Testament, made no bones about his sinful nature: *Surely I was sinful at birth, sinful from the time my mother conceived me* (Psalm 51:5). The apostle Paul is a towering New Testament figure, yet links himself with his readers and confesses that *Like the rest, we were by nature objects of wrath* (Ephesians 2:3).

Man is not a morally improved creature but a ruined one, and no manipulation of the biblical text can make it say otherwise. Visiting the famous Cunard liner *Queen Mary*, moored in Long Beach, California, I noticed that the mirrors in the staterooms were rose-tinted, so that when sailing in rough weather and feeling unwell, passengers looking in the mirrors would think they had a healthy glow! No such trickery is possible with the Bible, which shows sin in its true colours. It describes it as a stain, a rebellion, a poison, crookedness, a burden, a storm, wandering, a sickness, a disease, a field of weeds, darkness, blindness, bondage, a debt, robbery and a curse, and adds that if we deny our depravity 'we deceive ourselves and the truth is not in us'.

To minimize the nature and gravity of sin is not only foolish but fatal, as it removes any hope of our being cured. To be suffering from a terminal illness is serious, but not to know that this is the case, or to be in denial about it, makes the situation even worse. The person who does not realize or accept that he or she was born with a spiritual disease for which there is no human cure is in a truly desperate state. As the Bible ironically puts it, *It is not the healthy who need a doctor, but the sick* (Matthew 9:12).

The penalty

Our deliberate rebellion against God and his law has exposed us to his righteous anger and judgement, both in this world and in the world to come. The Bible warns us, *He who pursues evil goes to his death* (Provers 11:19), and in biblical terms 'death' means not only physical death, the separation of the soul from the body, but spiritual death, the eternal separation of the soul from God. We are destined to *die once, and after that to face judgement* (Hebrews 9:27) and, left to ourselves, our fate is *to be punished with everlasting destruction and shut out from the presence of the Lord and from the majesty of his power* (2 Thessalonians 1:9). The word the Bible most commonly uses for this is 'hell', and it leaves no doubt about its appalling reality. Jesus himself made it clear that those who reject the Bible's teaching will be *condemned to hell* (Matthew 23:33) and that it is a place of *torment* (Luke 16:28) and of *eternal punishment* (Matthew 25:46).

None of our own ethical, moral or religious efforts will do anything to cure our spiritual sickness or stave off God's judgement on us. In terms of making us right with God even our best efforts *are like filthy rags* (Isaiah 64:6). A car may have automatic transmission, power steering, cruise control, air conditioning and heated seats, but if the engine is wrecked it will go nowhere. In the same way, no amount of religious or social 'good' can make up for the fact that our hearts are *deceitful above all things and beyond cure* (Jeremiah 17:9) Left to ourselves, we are guilty, lost and helpless.

The good news

There is good news—news that nobody could possibly have invented—and it can be summed up in one sentence: *God so loved the world that he gave his one and only Son, that whoever believes in him shall not perish but have eternal life* (John 3:16). In an act of amazing love God dramatically intervened in the human disaster. In the person of Jesus, God the Son became a man and, although he himself was 'without sin', he chose to take upon himself the physical and spiritual death penalty on behalf of sinners. In his death on the cross he became as accountable for their sins as if he had been responsible for them. The only completely innocent human being in history agreed to suffer the double death penalty all other humans deserved. Jesus met the demands of God's law not only by obeying it in every part, but by paying in full the penalty it imposes on the disobedient.

Three days after he was put to death Jesus was *declared with power to be the Son of God by his resurrection from the dead* (Romans 1:4) and *Death no longer has mastery over him* (Romans 6:9) Jesus, the eternal Son of God, is alive today and *is able to save completely those who come to God through him* (Hebrews 7:25). There is more evidence (the Bible speaks of *many convincing proofs* in Acts 1:3) for the eternal resurrection of Jesus from the dead than for the Roman invasion of Britain about eighty years earlier. This evidence includes the testimonies of millions of people that he has transformed their lives, given them an assurance that their sins are forgiven and convinced them that after death they will by God's grace spend eternity with him in heaven, enjoying *an inheritance that can never perish, spoil or fade* (1 Peter 1:4).

Responding to the message

This is a brief summary of the Bible's storyline. The ball is now in the reader's court, so let me switch to the second person singular and ask what your response is. If you still reject what the Bible has to say, is it because you have read it all the way through with an open mind and have proved (at least to your own satisfaction) that it is flawed—*or because it says that you are*? As one author put it, 'If the Bible is actually God's voice to men, as it claims to be, then ... my opinion of the Bible is secondary to the Bible's opinion of me. What matters ultimately is not how I judge the Bible, but how its Author judges me.' Can you honestly say that there is no truth in the Bible's contention that you 'come short of the glory of God'? Have you never felt any need for God in your life? Have you given no thought to what might lie beyond the grave? Is this something on which you are prepared to take a chance? Does it make sense to reject God's offer of the forgiveness of sins and eternal life?

It may be that even after reading this booklet you find yourself saying, 'Prove to me that the Bible is true.' If so, my reply is this: 'Prove it for yourself!' It so happens that the central verse in the Authorized Version of the Bible, first published in 1611, is a perfect précis of its message: *It is better to trust in the Lord than to put confidence in man* (Psalm 118:8). Millions of people have tested this statement and found it to be true! You now have an opportunity to do the same. Sir Thomas Taylor, one-time Principal of Aberdeen University, wrote, 'Where the God of the Bible is concerned, men search for him in precisely the way that the average mouse searches for the average cat,' yet as God is *abounding in love*

(Psalm 86:5) and *not wanting anyone to perish, but everyone to come to repentance* (2 Peter 3:9) it would be impossible to imagine a more foolish response. Let me urge you not to make such a tragic mistake. Instead, come to the Bible as open-mindedly as you possibly can, asking God to make its message clear and personal and to give you the grace to respond as you should. You have nothing to lose and everything to gain. God says, *You will seek me and find me when you seek me with all your heart* (Jeremiah 29:13) — and he has yet to break a single promise!